International Labour Office

TRAINER TRAINING FOR LABOUR ADMINISTRATIONS

A practical guide

Robert Heron

ILO East Asia Multidisciplinary Advisory Team
ILO Regional Office for Asia and the Pacific
Bangkok

First published 1997

ISBN 92-2-110704-3

Printed in Thailand

Foreword

Ministries of labour in non-industrialized countries face a range of new challenges in providing a wide spectrum of labour services for the benefit of workers and employers. These challenges, however, and the work responsibilities they entail have not been accompanied by additional staff and material resources essential for effective performance.

Of particular concern to ministries of labour is the issue of staff resources. Frequently, they have insufficient staff to provide the range and quality of services required and the staff they do have lack training in modern approaches to labour administration and labour relations. They need to provide induction training for new staff members, and upgrading, refresher and specialist training for those already in service.

The lack of access to training courses relevant to the needs of labour officials makes it necessary for ministries of labour to plan, organize and conduct their own training activities using in-house resources. Reliance on internal resources requires the existence of labour officials trained as trainers, with the necessary competence to design training courses, prepare and present training sessions, and evaluate the effectiveness of their efforts.

This booklet provides a simple step-by-step approach to assist labour officials to develop their training capacity, thereby increasing their self-reliance in this most important area of work. It is part of an EASMAT series of guides on labour administration and industrial relations. As with other titles in this series, its translation into national languages is actively encouraged.

This booklet has been prepared by Robert Heron, Senior Labour Administration Specialist, with the assistance of Caroline Vandenabeele, Associate Expert in Labour Law and Industrial Relations, of the ILO East Asia Multidisciplinary Advisory Team.

W.R. Simpson
Director
ILO East Asia Multidisciplinary
Advisory Team (ILO/EASMAT)

Bangkok
August 1997

Table of contents

1

Introduction

You have been selected to be a trainer for your ministry, department or organization. To train others effectively you need to know:

- **what** you want them to know and do
- **how** to train them

What you want your participants to know and do will require detailed preparation on the subject matter of each training course you plan to conduct.

This guide concentrates on **how** to train others. This requires that you know:

- how to design a training course
- how to design and present a training session
- how to evaluate a training activity
- how to use a variety of training methods

The training process

Training is part of the change process. It involves bringing about changes in people to enable them to perform their work better.

Training provides people with new knowledge, skills and techniques and, perhaps, different attitudes to enable them to do new and different things, and to do existing tasks in different ways.

Training must relate to **real** needs, which must be properly assessed.

Training must be carefully planned if real needs are to be met.

Training is a continuous process rather than an isolated event. It should be provided on an ongoing basis.

Training is expensive, both in terms of direct and indirect costs (e.g. time taken). But it also brings benefits to the individual and his/her organization. Well-planned and properly implemented training produces benefits that exceed costs. It **can** be cost effective.

Training must consider not only the technical and professional needs of participants but also their needs as adult learners.

Training must be carefully planned if it is to address real needs.

3 Designing a training course

There is a difference between a training course and a training programme.

A **training programme** represents the overall programme or plan of training activities for a given period. It provides the essential guidance for **all** training activities in the organization.

A **training course** represents **one part** of the overall programme or plan and consists of a series of interrelated training sessions.

This guide is concerned with designing a training course, not an entire programme.

Designing a training course is part art and part science. It is an art in that it requires creativity and imagination. It is a science in that it involves the application of rules, procedures and techniques which, if followed, will produce predictable results.

A training course is a series of events which unfold to achieve a set of objectives.

In designing a training course we need to consider the following:

- Needs
- Goals, aims and objectives
- Content and subject matter
- Methodology
- Form
- Timetable
- Evaluation
- Appraisal

A. Needs

Needs are a reflection of a problem:

A hungry person needs food.

A sick person needs medical treatment.

Because there is a problem, **something** needs to be done. Sometimes, that something is training. But we must accept that some problems will not be solved by training alone. Indeed, they require new policies, procedures and equipment, and more staff.

But for the strengthening and development of labour administration and industrial relations, training **is** an important need. In order for labour officials to perform their duties to an acceptable level they must possess certain:

- knowledge
- skills
- personal qualities

These represent their needs. For you, as a trainer, it is necessary to **identify** these needs. You can do this in a number of ways:

- Ask labour officials what they think they need, either individually or in a group.
- Enquire from others what they think labour officials need.
- Observe labour officials in action.
- Conduct examinations to test labour officials' knowledge and skills, and use the results to highlight weaknesses and thus identify needs.
- Examine labour officials' performance reports.

An assessment of training needs should start with an analysis of the job description for a labour official and the job profile relating to that job description.

Example:

The work of a labour inspector requires:

(a) a detailed knowledge of labour laws and related regulations

(b) a knowledge of the production process

(c) the skills to communicate effectively with employers and workers

(d) the personal qualities of patience and impartiality

If through observation, self-assessment, examination, interviews, and discussion it is shown that the labour inspector lacks knowledge and skills in these areas, a training need has been identified.

When the labour inspector lacks the personal qualities of patience and impartiality, a need has been identified, but it will be more difficult to attend to this through training. It may be more a problem to be addressed in the recruitment and selection of inspectors.

B. Goals, aims and objectives

In planning a training course it is necessary to distinguish between:

- goals
- aims
- objectives

Goals are broad statements which refer to the overall purpose of training.

> " The goal of this training course is to strengthen labour administration services as a contribution to economic and social progress."

Aims are more specific than goals and refer to the changes in knowledge, skills and attitudes the training course is designed to achieve.

> " The aim of this training course is to provide labour officials with the knowledge and skills required to provide effective inspection services."

Objectives are specific statements of what participants will be able to do as a result of the training course:

> " By the end of the training course participants will be able to:
>
> (a) **outline** the main steps to follow in preparing for a routine inspection
>
> (b) **identify** the main stages in conducting a routine inspection
>
> (c) **identify** the obstacles and constraints in providing effective inspection services"

A clear set of objectives helps:

- the trainer
- participants
- the organization

It helps the **trainer** to:

- select the subject matter for the course
- decide on the length and form of the course
- decide on suitable learning methods
- select resource persons

It helps **participants** by:

- indicating what is expected of them during the course
- indicating what benefits they can expect from the course
- eliminating unrealistic expectations
- reinforcing their motivation to participate in the course

It helps the **organization** by:

- keeping those not directly engaged in training informed of what is going on
- providing a basis for seeing whether training activities are consistent with policy guidelines

GOALS

AIMS

OBJECTIVES

C. Content and subject matter

Once the goals, aims and objectives have been established you can decide on the course content.

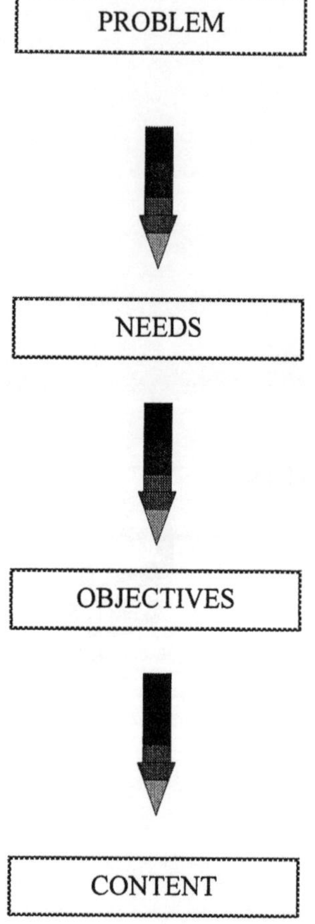

The content falls into three categories:

- that which is essential and **must** be included
- that which is useful and **should** be included
- that which is marginal and **might** be included

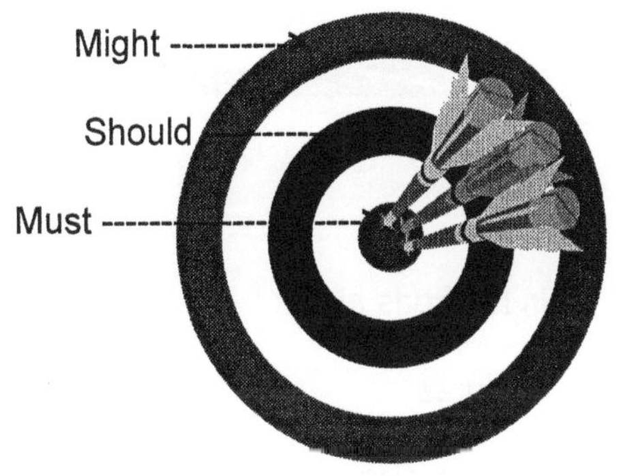

Example:

What must, should or might be included in a basic training course on labour administration?

- Knowledge of ILO Conventions on labour administration?

- Knowledge of the inspection process?

- Knowledge of the collective bargaining process?

- Skills in handling confrontational situations?

- Skills in conciliation and mediation?

- Knowledge of national labour laws?

- Knowledge of national employment policies?

D. Methodology

In designing your training course, it is necessary to consider which methods to use to enable learning to take place.

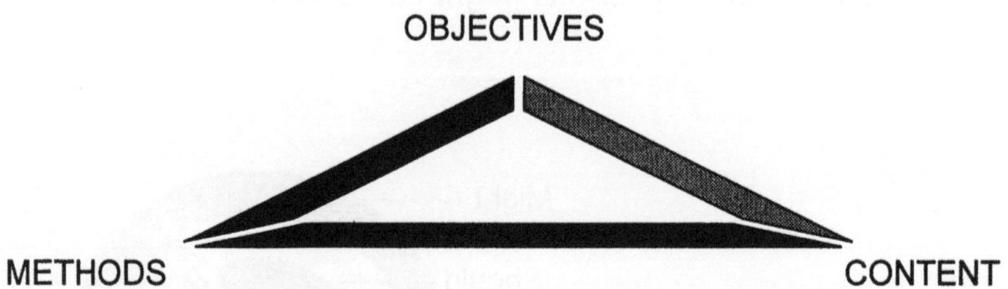

The main methods are:

- lectures
- lecture-discussions
- discussions
- case-studies
- role-plays

These methods can be supported by various **training media** (e.g. films, videos, slides) and **activities** (e.g. field visits, study attachments).

The methods you select should take account of the fact that participants in training courses in labour administration and industrial relations will be adults. Their needs as labour officials will determine the content of the training course; their needs as adult learners will determine the methodology.

E. Form

The form or format of a training course refers to the way in which it is structured and organized. Some of the forms are given below:

- Training course
- Seminar
- Workshop
- Study tour
- Distance learning
- Sandwich course, involving periods of training as part of the work cycle

The form of the course should be influenced largely by its objectives, but also by the availability of funds, premises (e.g. training rooms and facilities) and resource persons.

Try to choose the form that is best rather than easiest.

F. Timetable

The content or subject matter of the course must be structured in some way. It may consist of a series of lectures on a number of related topics or, alternatively, problem situations designed to provide a focus for learning to take place.

The training course needs to be divided into a number of parts, usually referred to as sessions. These should be arranged to stress:

- **continuity** - the order in which sessions are presented to enable one session to flow logically into another.

  Example:

  It would be better to have a session on employment policies before a session on the purpose and functions of public employment services.

- **sequence** - the order in which the subject material is presented in relation to the learning needs of participants.

  Example:

  It would be easier for participants to know what inspection is (instruction) before they are shown how to do it (application).

- **integration** - all sessions should fit together and contribute to achieving the objectives of the course. Thus, the objectives are the integrating force for any training course.

  Example:

  A course concerned with developing conciliation skills would not normally include a session on the role of public employment services as this does not integrate with the course objectives.

In drawing up your timetable:

- set aside time at the beginning to create a suitable learning climate
- allow time for review sessions
- provide for breaks and rest periods
- don't make the sessions too long
- provide time for participants to exchange information, ideas and experiences, and to ask questions
- alternate information-giving sessions (lectures) with activities, tasks and exercises
- schedule key sessions when participants are fresh and concentration levels high
- avoid scheduling heavy sessions at times when participants are likely to be tired

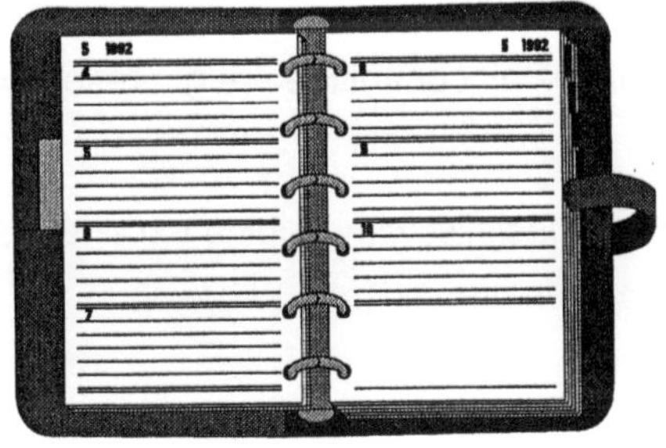

PLAN CAREFULLY

WHAT TO DO AND

WHEN TO DO IT

G. Evaluation

In designing your course you will need to give careful thought to how it will be evaluated.

Evaluation is concerned with comparing actual with planned outcomes. Although it usually takes place at the end of each session or course, you will have to plan how you will do it **before** the session or course commences.

H. Appraisal

Once you have designed your training course, it should be subject to some form of appraisal before it commences.

Appraisal is concerned with comparing the estimated benefits of the training to be provided with its estimated costs. As a result, we may decide to change the design of the course, reduce the budget or not to continue.

A training course can be appraised by:

- presenting your course proposal to colleagues for comment
- presenting your proposal to a committee (e.g. resource committee)
- drawing on the services of a specialist with training experience

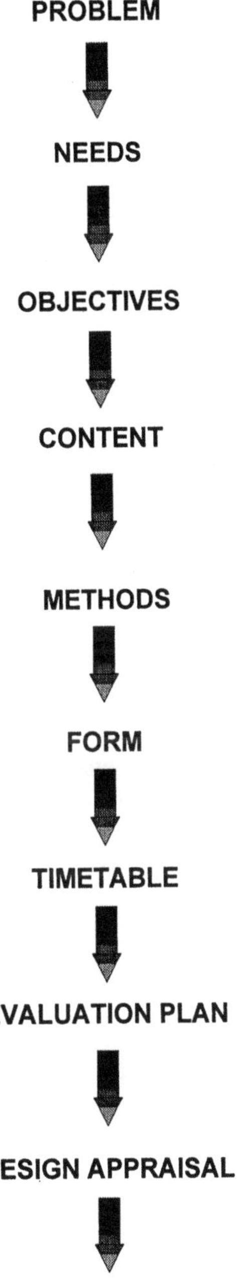
PROBLEM
NEEDS
OBJECTIVES
CONTENT
METHODS
FORM
TIMETABLE
EVALUATION PLAN
DESIGN APPRAISAL
IMPLEMENTATION

Designing a training session

A training course consists of a number of sessions. Each training session will have to be properly planned and well presented if it is to contribute effectively to the course.

Your training session will have:

- an aim
- some specific objectives
- a specific subject matter
- a proper structure
- a time sequence

In planning your session you will need to consider the methods you will use to ensure the objectives are achieved to the highest possible degree.

A. Aim

The aim of your training session will highlight the knowledge and information you wish to convey to the participants.

> Example:
>
> The aim of this training session is to provide participants with a knowledge of the relevant sections of the labour law of concern to labour inspectors.

The aim lacks specific detail, but provides general guidance to you, as a trainer, and to course participants to enable the session to be focused and 'on track'.

B. Objectives

The objectives refer to the specific things you expect participants to be able to do after the session is over.

Example:

By the end of this session participants will be able to:

(a) **define** labour administration

(b) **identify** the relevant sections of the labour law concerning labour administration

(c) **outline** the main functional responsibilities of labour administrators

(d) **identify** their role in the provision of labour administration services

In stating the objectives you should avoid such statements as: "By the end of the session participants will be effective labour administrators." This is far too ambitious an objective for one training session. The best you can hope for is that participants will have gained the necessary knowledge and information concerning the work of labour administrators. Whether they can apply this to practical work situation will depend on further training sessions and the opportunity to apply the knowledge acquired.

C. Subject matter

The subject matter refers to the actual information to be presented during the training session.

- Concentrate on a subject matter which is essential rather than marginal.
- What is essential depends on the specific objectives of the training session.
- The subject matter should focus on the needs of participants, not on the preferences of the trainer.
- In selecting the subject matter be aware of the time limits. It is better to cover a few key matters very well, rather than attempt to present a large amount of information in a superficial manner.

D. The structure

The session consists of three parts:

- A beginning
- A middle
- An end

The beginning

In the start of your session you must gain the attention of participants and prepare them for what will follow.

- Make clear to participants what they will learn in this session.
- Indicate **why** this session is important.
- Relate the beginning to what has happened in previous sessions of the same course.

  Example:

  "In our previous sessions we looked at labour administration in general terms. In this session we will look particularly at labour inspection as a means of improving the conditions of employment and the working environment. By the end of this session it is expected you will be able to..."

In the beginning,
say what you are going to say.

The middle

The middle consists of the real substance of your session. This is where you provide the information and ideas that will enable your objectives to be achieved.

- Arrange the content of your session in such a way that it unfolds in a logical order.
- Present your material in easy-to-absorb portions.
- Use examples to illustrate the information you wish to convey.

In the beginning,
say what you are going to say.

In the middle,
say it.

The end

Your session has to come to an end. Rather than abruptly say: "I have finished", take a few minutes to review and summarize the main points of your session and indicate the really important things you want participants to recall and think about.

Example:

" In this session we have talked about the nature of labour inspection and identified the main sections of the labour law which refer to the work of inspectors. We are now more aware of what inspectors are required to do but this, of course, does not make us effective inspectors in practice. In our next session we will look at some of the skills and techniques used by inspectors which will build on the knowledge provided in this current session. Thank you."

In the beginning,
you say what you are going to say.

In the middle,
you say it.

At the end,
say what you have said.

E. Time sequence

It is necessary to plan your time to ensure that you concentrate on the really important things.

- Prepare a session plan.
- Write down your aims and objectives.
- Indicate how much time you will spend on the beginning, middle and end.
- Indicate the main parts of the middle (body) of your presentation, and the time to be spent on each part.

Example of a session plan:

Title: The legal framework for employment services.

Duration: 60 minutes

Aim: To provide participants with a knowledge of the relevant sections of the labour law relating to employment services.

Objectives: By the end of this session participants will be able to:

(a) **indicate** the purpose and functions of employment services

(b) **identify** the relevant sections of the labour law concerning employment services

(c) **outline** the main provisions of these relevant sections

(d) **identify** their role in the implementation of these sections

Content:

Beginning/introduction (5 minutes)

Middle/body (50 minutes)

End/conclusion (5 minutes)

F. Methods

The methods chosen for the session should meet two criteria:

- They should ensure that the subject matter is taught in such a way to achieve the stated objectives to the maximum possible degree.
- They should recognize the needs of participants as adult learners.

The needs of your participants as labour administrators will influence the *content* of your session.

Their needs as adult learners will influence the *methods* for your session.

You should decide whether your method should be:

- trainer dominated
- trainer centred
- learner centred

You should vary the methods of presentation. For some parts of your presentation you will need to dominate and simply give information (lecture or trainer dominated). For certain parts you may wish to encourage discussions on the information and ideas you have presented (trainer centred). For other parts, and depending on the time available, you may wish to have participants discuss issues amongst themselves (learner centred).

5 Presenting your session

Much of the success of your session will depend on how you actually present it.

Effective presentation is effective communication. This requires you to:

- organize and structure what you say before you say it
- develop your communication skills to minimize the possibility of a failure of communication

A. Verbal communication

- Speak slowly and clearly.
- Vary the tone of your voice.
- Refrain from technical language unless you are sure it will be understood.
- Do not use colloquial expressions.
- Avoid words with hidden or double meanings.

Speak slowly and clearly.

B. Non-verbal communication

You will use more than words to convey information and ideas. Body movements and facial expressions are part of the communication process.

- Maintain eye contact with your participants.
- Avoid making irritating gestures.
- Use gestures which reinforce what you are saying.
- Control your facial expressions.
- Adopt a suitable posture.
- Refrain from making sounds which are not real words (e.g. ah, um).

To be an effective presenter you do NOT need to develop a new voice or vocabulary or change your looks.

BE YOURSELF

Your participants will make judgements on your presentation, which will include the following:

- Was the presenter well prepared?
- Were the objectives of the course clear?
- Did the session have a proper structure - a beginning, middle, end?
- Were the actual words used suitable? Was the language too simple? Was it too technical?
- Was the voice suitable? Was it too loud? Was it too soft? Was it too monotonous?
- Were the posture and manner appropriate? Were body movements natural? Was eye contact maintained? Did facial expressions assist in conveying the message?
- Was the presenter relaxed and natural?
- Did the speaker manage the available time carefully?

If you consider these questions when you prepare your presentation, there is every possibility it will be better as a result.

C. Visual aids

Your presentation should be supported by various visual aids. You need to let your participants **see** what you are saying to reinforce what they hear.

The two most commonly used visual aids are:

- the blackboard/whiteboard or flip chart
- the overhead projector

When using a **blackboard/whiteboard** or **flipchart**:

- write clearly
- make sure that your writing is large enough to be seen by all
- organize the material you present to make full use of the space available
- use what you write to illustrate and clarify what you are saying

Very little learning takes place if participants simply copy material from the board or flipchart.

When using an **overhead projector**:

- check that the equipment is working before you start your presentation
- prepare your transparencies by keeping a margin (2-3 cm) on all sides
- print rather than write on the transparencies
- do not write too much on a transparency (20-30 words is sufficient)
- use the transparencies to assist your presentation - they are not meant to replace it
- do not look at or point to the screen when illustrating a point on the transparency; maintain eye contact with the audience

6 Briefing visiting session leaders

As a trainer, you will not be expected to conduct every session in a course yourself. Sometimes you will utilize visiting lecturers. It is your responsibility, as a trainer, to ensure that the visitor is properly briefed and able to prepare a good session plan.

You should provide them with information on:

- why the session is included in the course
- the specific objectives of the session
- the subject matter to be covered
- the number and background of participants (experience, education level, language ability)
- the length of the session
- where the session will be held
- the availability of items such as overhead projector, flip chart, slide projector and microphone
- whether they will be required to answer questions

Evaluating a training activity

Evaluation means:

- making assessments
- judging work or quality
- measuring results

The three basic elements of evaluation are:

- measurement
- comparison
- judgement

Measurement means taking measures of performance.

Examples:

45% in a mathematics examination
500 workdays lost in a dispute
1,200 work accidents in a year

Comparison means relating the actual measures of performance to an agreed standard.

Example:

50% is the pass mark for the mathematics examination.

Judgement means making decisions and interpretations based on the comparison of actual with planned results.

Example:

45% in mathematics constitutes failure.

STANDARD

MEASURES

COMPARISON

JUDGEMENT

ACTION

The evaluation process involves:

- collecting information
- analysing information
- making comparisons
- making judgements
- taking action

As a trainer, you can evaluate:

- the entire course
- each individual session
- the participants
- the methods used

Most of your evaluation efforts will concentrate on evaluating the entire course or the participants.

You will evaluate your **training course** to find out:

- whether the course has achieved its stated objectives
- how to improve the course if it is to be conducted again
- whether the cost of the course has been justified
- how the trainers involved can perform better in the future

You will evaluate **course participants** to find out:

- their reaction to the course
- what they have learned during the course

A. Types of evaluation

Reaction evaluation concentrates on finding out what participants **feel** about the course. It is based on their **opinions** which are obtained from questionnaires, interviews, discussions and observations.

Learning evaluation concentrates on finding out the **learning** which has taken place as a result of the course. This usually involves a written test, but may include a more practical test in which participants are required to do something.

In addition to reaction and learning evaluations, as a trainer you will also be interested in **performance** and **impact evaluation**.

Performance evaluation concentrates on finding out whether the training course has improved on-the-job performance. This is usually done some months after the training course.

Impact evaluation concentrates on finding out whether the training provided has had a positive effect on the organization, as a whole, and whether the course has contributed to solving the problems it was designed to overcome.

The difference between reaction, learning, performance and impact evaluation is illustrated below:

Example:

Conciliators find that there is a large backlog of cases to handle and they are falling behind in their work. It is thought that the problem is due to a lack of training for conciliators. As a result, a training course is conducted to provide conciliators with new knowledge and skills.

A **reaction evaluation** for this course would ascertain whether the conciliators found the training to be worthwhile by asking for their opinions.

A **learning evaluation** would require the conciliators to complete a written test or to demonstrate their knowledge and skills in a practical test.

A **performance evaluation** would require the conciliators to apply their knowledge and skills on the job and for them to be assessed on their actual work performance.

An **impact evaluation** would assess whether the training course was successful in overcoming the problem of the backlog of cases. If it is found, in spite of the training, the backlog of cases remains the same or increases, the training has had no real impact or ultimate result because the original problem remains.

B. Methods of evaluation

Evaluation may be either formal or informal.

Formal methods of evaluation:

- Questionnaires
- Written or oral examinations
- Self-assessment, using a checklist
- Assessment by an independent observer
- Structured interviews with individual participants
- Interviews with groups of participants

Informal methods of evaluation:

- Observation of participants' progress.
- Conversations with individual participants
- Discussions with small groups of participants
- Personal reflection

8 Training methods

The main training methods are:

- lectures
- lecture-discussions
- group discussions
- role-plays
- case-studies

A. Lectures

This method relies on one-way communication and is essentially a trainer-dominated approach. The lecturer speaks and participants listen. Unless the lecturer is extremely skilled or makes good use of effective visual aids, the learning which takes place under this method is questionable.

The advantages of this method are:

- a large amount of material can be presented in a short time
- large groups can be addressed.

The lecture method is best used to introduce new information and ideas, followed by opportunities for questions and discussions.

B. Lecture-discussions

This is an interactive method in that periods of lecture are interspersed with time for reactions, questions, comments and discussions.

This approach is trainer centred but not trainer dominated. It has the advantages of enabling the trainer to:

- present information and ideas to participants
- gather information and ideas from participants

Although there can be a high degree of participation and interaction in this type of session, the trainer retains control of the process and outcomes.

This method draws on the trainer's questioning and listening skills. The trainer should try to ask 'open questions'; these cannot be answered by 'yes' or 'no' and have no right or wrong answer. They encourage participants to think about an issue and then speak.

You, as a trainer, listen to their responses and build on them by asking further questions or encouraging less active participants to respond and participate in the discussion.

In a lecture-discussion session, you convey information and ideas, collect reactions and ideas from participants, and work with them to bring order and structure to the information provided.

C. Group discussions

In group discussions you change your approach from trainer centred to learner centred. You become more of a facilitator and surrender control of the session to the group in an atmosphere of cooperative learning.

Group discussions have the advantage of:

- flexibility - they can be designed as full sessions in themselves or be included as part of a wider discussion
- requiring minimal training aids and equipment

Group discussions have the disadvantage of:

- not being suitable for providing new information
- sometimes being difficult to manage
- taking up a large amount of time
- leading to outcomes different from those planned

There are three main types of discussion groups used by trainers:

- guided discussion groups
- syndicate groups
- buzz groups

Guided discussion groups

In this group arrangement you, as a trainer, pose a question or problem, or present a theme for discussion. You would normally guide discussions by asking occasional questions, using prompter statements and summing up at suitable intervals.

You do not dominate discussions but attempt to manage them in relation to the theme or issue under discussion. The major contributions and outcomes are provided by the participants.

The effectiveness of this method depends, in part, on the size of the group; it works well for groups of 10-12 participants.

The best results will be achieved when you:

- choose a topic likely to be of interest to everyone
- provide the group with sufficient information
- ensure the issue to be discussed is clearly understood
- select a topic with a number of points of view
- have the knowledge and skills to lead the group

As a discussion group leader you should:

- have clear objectives
- prepare questions and prompter statements
- listen carefully
- know the subject
- be able to summarize
- encourage all in the group to participate
- respect the viewpoints of others

Syndicate groups

In this type of group discussion you divide participants into groups of five or six and ask each group to reflect on a theme, problem or question. The groups are not supervised by the trainer: you exercise control by the way in which the questions or problems are stated and by the instructions you provide.

Once discussions commence, the way in which they are conducted and the outcomes are no longer in your hands.

Syndicate groups provide an opportunity for participants to express views without the involvement of the trainer. The 'risk' is that discussions may lack focus and get sidetracked.

Buzz groups

These are small groups, usually of two or three persons, set up as part of a lecture-discussion session. Participants are asked to discuss a particular issue or share experiences, usually for a short period (e.g. 3-10 minutes).

You can use these group discussions to help participants get their thoughts together before taking part in a longer discussion. They can also be used to break up a lecture by allowing participants to discuss a problem or issue related to the theme of that lecture.

Buzz groups provide an opportunity for every participant to engage in discussions and make your training sessions more lively.

D. Role-plays

Role-playing is a technique that requires participants to act out a problem or situation. As actors, they usually do something different from their normal situation.

Role-playing has the advantages of:

- bringing reality to the training room
- serving as a bridge between theory and practice
- allowing participants to practice new skills in the safety of the training room where mistakes can be made and corrected
- providing an opportunity for participants to learn from the behaviour of others

Role-playing involves three stages:

- Preparation
- Conduct
- Conclusion

Preparation

You, as a trainer, should create a situation that is suitable for interaction, and then describe this situation in writing (e.g. conducting an inspection, interviewing a jobseeker, dismissing a worker).

You will need to give written instructions to participants indicating what is expected of them.

Conduct

Before the role-playing actually commences you should:

- check the materials, equipment and furniture required
- issue instructions, both written and oral
- stress the learning objectives of the exercise
- reassure those participants who are anxious or reluctant to play their allocated roles
- set time-limits
- inform participants you will intervene in the role-play if it is ‘going off the rails’

Part of conducting the role-play involves providing participants with the opportunity to prepare themselves for their roles. They will need time to study the actual problem and consider the instructions you have given; at least 30 minutes preparation time is required for most structured role-plays. It is also possible to conduct unstructured role-plays which require participants to interact spontaneously, without time for preparation.

The action for the role-play sees the actors in position, acting out their respective roles. The trainer gives up control to the actors, but should be prepared to stop the role-play if it is not contributing to the proposed learning outcomes.

Those participants who are not acting are assigned the role of observers. They will be given an opportunity to comment on their observations once the role-play is finished.

SOME PARTICIPANTS WILL BE ACTORS,

THE REST WILL BE OBSERVERS.

Conclusion

Once the acting phase is over, it is necessary to use the role-play experience to show the learning that has taken place. This involves giving a chance to the actors to talk about their experiences during the role-play, to the observers to share their observations, and to you to offer your comments and, generally, slowly leading participants away from the experience of acting to the reality of the learning that has taken place.

Role-playing involves acting, but this is not an end in itself. Its real purpose is to use the acting experience to encourage learning.

E. Case-studies

Case-studies represent a way of providing focused learning either individually or in groups. They enable participants to sharpen their problem-solving skills and to share ideas and experiences.

When used in relation to group discussions, there are four main aspects to case-studies:

- preparation
- discussion
- presentation
- review

Preparation

The case-study should be written and preferably relate to a real-life situation. It should give the background to the issue (location, fictional names, legal context) and provide sufficient information for participants to identify the real problem to be solved.

The case-study should be introduced to participants by providing an overview of the key issues, answering their questions and generally clarifying their task.

Participants should be given some instruction on an acceptable approach to problem solving. They should be advised to:

- identify the facts
- analyse those facts and identify related issues
- determine the real problem and subproblems
- consider various alternative approaches to solving each problem
- provide a preferred solution (which might be a combination of various alternatives)

Discussion

The discussion of the case-study will follow the format of the syndicate groups outlined above. The actual discussions are not supervised by the trainer; the only real control you have over the discussions will depend on the instructions and guidance provided at the preparation stage.

Presentation

Each syndicate group should be provided with an opportunity to present the outcome of its discussions to the entire group. This presentation should concentrate on the identification of the **real** problem and the **alternative approaches** to solving this problem.

The whole group should be invited to respond to the presentation by asking questions and challenging the conclusions reached. The presenting group should be provided with an opportunity to clarify its position and defend its arguments.

Review

On conclusion of the case-study discussions and presentations, the trainer should review the entire activity to highlight outcomes in relation to the learning objectives as originally established.

Individual case-studies

Rather than have the case-study discussed by syndicate groups, it is possible for the exercise to be undertaken on an individual basis. This would mean that each individual would make a written response to the case-study, which would then be the subject of individual comments by the trainer. This approach is more demanding on the trainer's time and provides no opportunity for group interaction to elaborate the various issues.

www.ingramcontent.com/pod-product-compliance
Ingram Content Group UK Ltd.
Pitfield, Milton Keynes, MK11 3LW, UK
UKHW041849190726
13854UKWH00002B/792